All you need to know about Vietnam

Copyright © 2024 Jonas Hoffmann-Schmidt.
Translation: Linda Amber Chambers.

All rights reserved. This book, including all its parts, is protected by copyright. Any use outside the narrow limits of copyright law is prohibited without the written consent of the author. This book has been created using artificial intelligence to provide unique and informative content.

Disclaimer: This book is for entertainment purposes only. The information, facts and views contained therein have been researched and compiled to the best of our knowledge and belief. Nevertheless, the author and the publisher assume no liability for the accuracy or completeness of the information. Readers should consult with professionals before making any decisions based on this information. Use of this book is the responsibility of the reader.

Introduction 6

Geography and climate of Vietnam 9

Early history of Vietnam 12

The Era of Chinese Rule 14

The independence movements and the Đinh dynasty 16

The Lý Dynasty and the heyday of Vietnam 18

The Tran and Hồ Dynasties 20

The Le Dynasty and the Era of the Nguyen Lords 22

French colonial rule 24

The Vietnamese resistance against the colonial power 27

The Partition of Vietnam: The Vietnam War 30

Reunification and the Socialist Republic of Vietnam 33

Political system and current developments 36

Economy and trade in Vietnam 39

Education and health care 42

Art & Literature in Vietnam 44

Music and traditional Vietnamese instruments 47

Religions in Vietnam: Buddhism, Catholicism and folk religions 49

Daily life in Vietnam 51

Traditional clothing and fashion 54

Vietnamese cuisine: flavours and influences 57

National dishes of Vietnam 60

Street food and local delicacies 62

Vietnam's wildlife: from the red river dolphin to the Javan rhinoceros 64

Nature conservation and environmental problems 67

Hanoi: capital and cultural center 70

Ho Chi Minh City (Saigon): Economic heart of Vietnam 73

Huế: The Imperial City on the Perfume River 76

Hội An: The Historic Trade Center 79

Dalat: The City of Flowers and Eternal Spring 81

Halong Bay: A UNESCO World Heritage Site 84

The temple city of My Son 87

The Tunnels of Củ Chi 90

The Mekong Delta Region: Life in the River 93

The beaches of Phú Quốc and Nha Trang 96

The traditional Tet festival: Vietnamese New Year 98

The Art of Water Puppet Theatre 100

The Bat-Trang pottery: craft traditions 102

Language and script in Vietnam 104

Travel preparation and useful tips 106

Closing remarks 110

Introduction

The introduction to Vietnam is a journey through a fascinating history, rich culture and breathtaking landscapes. Geographically located in Southeast Asia, Vietnam borders China to the north, Laos and Cambodia to the west, and the South China Sea to the east. With a population of over 95 million people, Vietnam is a country of diversity, both in its scenic features and in its ethnic and cultural composition.

The history of Vietnam spans several millennia and is characterized by a unique development from the ancient kingdom to the modern socialist republic. The early Vietnamese civilization flourished along the Red River and the Mekong Delta, where people developed on rice paddies and waterways that still form the backbone of Vietnamese agriculture today.

Vietnam's history is also marked by alternating phases of independence and submission to foreign rule. From Chinese domination over centuries to colonization by the French in the 19th century, Vietnam has developed a rich tradition of resistance and cultural preservation. The Vietnam War, which raged from 1955 to 1975, marked a profound turning point in the country's modern history, with far-reaching political, social, and economic implications.

Culturally, Vietnam is known for its rich tradition in art, music, literature and architecture. From the ancient temples of Hue to the colonial mansions of Hanoi and the bustling markets of Ho Chi Minh City, Vietnam's architecture reflects the various influences that have shaped the country throughout its history. Vietnamese cuisine, famous for its freshness, variety and complex flavors, is one of the most popular in the world and attracts visitors from all corners of the globe.

Naturally, Vietnam offers an incredible variety of landscapes, from the mountain ranges in the north to the tropical beaches in the south. Halong Bay, a UNESCO World Heritage Site, is known for its emerald waters and limestone rock formations, while the Mekong Delta is a lush landscape of rice paddies and waterways.

In recent decades, Vietnam has become an emerging economic power in Southeast Asia, with industry and tourism being key drivers of growth. The population, which is increasingly urbanized, faces challenges in terms of environmental protection, social justice and economic development.

This introduction offers a first glimpse of the complexity and beauty of Vietnam, a country that honors its past while striving for the future. In the following chapters, we will dive deeper into the different facets of this fascinating country, from its history to its culture to its modern dynamism and unique traditions.

Geography and climate of Vietnam

Vietnam, located in Southeast Asia, stretches along the eastern coast of the Indochina Peninsula. The country is bordered by China to the north, Laos and Cambodia to the west, and the South China Sea to the south. With a total area of about 331,000 square kilometers, Vietnam is a diverse country that is geographically divided into three main regions.

In the north, mountainous areas dominate the landscape. The Hoheinzon stretches along the Chinese border and forms a natural barrier between Vietnam and its northern neighbor. Some of the highest peaks in the country can be found here, including Fan Si Pan, which is the highest mountain in Indochina at over 3,100 meters. The mountain ranges are often covered by dense forests that are rich in biodiversity and provide habitat for rare animal species such as the Red Panda.

The central region of Vietnam is characterized by the Annamite Mountains, which stretch from northwest to southeast. These mountains are less high than those in the north, but also offer an impressive landscape with deep valleys and dense forests. It is also home to the historic city of Huế, once the country's capital and now known for its imperial architecture, which is a UNESCO World Heritage Site.

The south of Vietnam, where the Mekong Delta is located, is mainly flat and crisscrossed by a number of rivers and canals. The Mekong Delta is one of the most fertile regions in the country and a center of agricultural production, especially for rice. The landscape here is characterized by lush rice paddies, orchards, and floating markets that define the lives of the people along the river.

The climate of Vietnam varies depending on the region. The north experiences a subtropical climate with four well-defined seasons, including a cold winter and a hot summer. The central region is tropical and characterized by monsoons, which occur during the rainy season from September to December. The south has a tropical savannah climate with high temperatures and a pronounced rainy season from May to October.

Vietnam's geographical diversity is reflected not only in its landscape, but also in its rich flora and fauna. The coastal waters provide habitat for a wide variety of marine life, while the country's dense forests are home to a variety of flora and fauna, including many endemic species.

Overall, Vietnam presents a fascinating combination of mountain ranges, fertile plains and tropical coastlines that not only make up its scenic beauty, but also strongly influence the way of life and culture of its population. The country's geographical diversity is an integral part of its identity and its appeal to visitors from all over the world.

Early history of Vietnam

The early history of Vietnam spans thousands of years and is characterized by a variety of cultural and civilizational developments. The first human traces in the region date back to the Paleolithic Age, about 500,000 years ago. At that time, the ancestors of today's Vietnamese lived as hunter-gatherers in the fertile valleys along the rivers that run through the country.

The Bronze Age, which began around 2000 BC, marked a significant step forward in the development of Vietnamese society. During this period, people began to make bronze tools and weapons, which led to an increase in agricultural productivity and the emergence of urban settlements. The Dong Son culture, named after an archaeological site in northern Vietnam, was one of the earliest advanced civilizations in the region and is known for its advanced bronze and ceramic production as well as its complex burial rituals.

From the 1st millennium BC, Vietnam was increasingly influenced by Chinese civilization, especially through trade and cultural exchange across the borders of the Red River. The Chinese Han Dynasty exercised considerable cultural and political dominance, which led to the establishment of a Chinese presence in the region and forced Vietnamese rulers to pay tribute.

The period between the 1st and 10th centuries AD was marked by a period of political change and cultural assimilation. Vietnam's independence efforts were reinforced by adapting to Chinese administrative methods and adopting Buddhist and Confucian ideas. Nevertheless, Vietnam retained its cultural identity and developed a unique synthesis of Chinese influence and indigenous traditions.

The period of Chinese rule ended in the 10th century, when Vietnamese rulers successfully declared independence from the Tang Dynasty and the country entered the feudal system of the Dinh Dynasty. This era was characterized by a strong centralization of political power and a heyday of literature, art, and architecture, leading to the rise of cities like Hanoi as cultural and political centers.

The early history of Vietnam is a history of change, adaptation and cultural exchange, which laid the foundation for the country's later development. Through the influence of different civilizations and the emergence of local dynasties, a rich cultural tradition was formed, which to this day shapes Vietnam's identity and enriches the understanding of its history.

The Era of Chinese Rule

The era of Chinese rule over Vietnam spanned several centuries and left a lasting influence on the political, cultural and social development of the country. The beginning of this era can be dated to the 2nd century BC, when the Chinese Empire under the Han Dynasty began to expand its power over the southern territories. The expansion to the south was aimed at securing trade routes and natural resources, as well as involving the local peoples in the tributary system of the Han Dynasty.

Vietnam, then known as Giao Chỉ, was incorporated into three southern provinces of the Chinese Empire, adopting Chinese administrative methods and legal norms. This led to the establishment of a Chinese presence in the region, including the stationing of officials and the establishment of administrative structures based on the Chinese hierarchy.

During Chinese rule, Vietnam experienced an increasing assimilation of Chinese culture and ideas. Chinese language and writing were introduced and served as a means of administration and education. Confucian philosophy and Buddhist teachings gained prominence and influenced the country's intellectual and religious landscape.

However, resistance to Chinese rule was pervasive, especially among local rulers and tribal leaders, who regularly organized uprisings to defend independence and undermine Chinese control. These resistance movements, although often suppressed, showed the deep-rooted independence mentality of the Vietnamese people and laid the foundation for later efforts for national unity and sovereignty.

Over time, the Chinese presence in Vietnam fluctuated, depending on the strength and stability of each Chinese dynasty. During periods of weakness or civil wars in China, Vietnam was able to temporarily restore its independence or enjoy some autonomy. Nevertheless, the tributary system remained in place until the mid-10th century, when Vietnam finally declared its independence under the Đinh dynasty and finally shook off Chinese rule.

The era of Chinese rule was a period of challenge and adaptation for Vietnam, producing both cultural synthesis and resistance to foreign domination. The experiences during this period shaped the national identity and helped to lay the foundation for the later development of an independent Vietnamese state.

The independence movements and the Đinh dynasty

The era of independence movements and the Đinh dynasty mark a significant period in Vietnam's history, marked by the struggle for national unity and the consolidation of an independent government. After centuries of Chinese rule and tributary status, Vietnam rose to a new political power in the 10th century under the Đinh dynasty.

The Đinh Dynasty was founded by Đinh Bộ Lĩnh, a military leader who opposed Chinese control of Vietnam and successfully united local tribes and rulers to establish an independent kingdom. Under his rule, the Đinh dynasty focused on strengthening central government and enforcing laws and administrative structures based on Vietnamese traditions.

A significant event during the Đinh Dynasty was the conquest of the Chinese protectorate in 938 AD, when Vietnamese troops defeated the Chinese garrisons and proclaimed the country's independence. This victory marked a turning point in Vietnam's history and laid the foundation for the later development of an independent state.

The Đinh dynasty ruled only for a short time, until 980 AD, when it was replaced by the Lê dynasty. Nevertheless, it left a lasting influence on the political organization and territorial unity of Vietnam. Under the Đinh dynasty, important infrastructure projects such as the construction of fortresses and the improvement of municipal administration began to promote national defense and economic development.

During their brief reign, the Đinh dynasty also focused on promoting education and literature. The Vietnamese language and culture were promoted, leading to a heyday of Vietnamese literature and poetry. This cultural upsurge helped to strengthen a unified national identity and weld the Vietnamese people closer together.

The Đinh Dynasty and the subsequent Lê Dynasty laid the foundation for Vietnam's further development as an independent nation, increasingly distancing itself from the influences of its Chinese neighbors and forming its own cultural and political identity. The experiences of this period left a lasting mark on Vietnam's history and paved the way for future dynasties and political developments that shaped the country until the modern era.

The Lý Dynasty and the heyday of Vietnam

The Lý Dynasty was an important period in Vietnam's history, marking a period of political stability, cultural flourishing and territorial expansion. The dynasty was founded in 1009 AD by Lý Thái Tổ, a general who successfully overthrew the Lê dynasty and declared himself emperor. Under his leadership and that of his successors, Vietnam developed into a flourishing civilization that prospered both internally and externally.

One of the most significant achievements of the Lý dynasty was the strengthening of central government and the implementation of effective administrative structures. This allowed for improved control over the territory and promoted economic development through the expansion of trade and agriculture. The dynasty also established a series of legal reforms aimed at equality and fairness and helped stabilize society.

Culturally, the Lý dynasty was a time of innovation and progress. Supported by a rich intellectual tradition, art, literature and architecture were promoted, leading to a heyday of Vietnamese culture. Temples and pagodas were built, including the famous One

Pillar Pagoda in Hanoi, which remains a significant landmark to this day.

The Lý rule was also marked by the promotion of Buddhism, which gained influence during this period and became an integral part of Vietnamese society. Buddhist monasteries were built, and monks played an important role in the country's spiritual and cultural development.

The foreign policy of the Lý dynasty was characterized by expansion to the south, which expanded Vietnamese territory. This led to the integration of areas in central and southern Vietnam and strengthened Vietnam's position as a regional power factor. Trade relations with China, India and other Asian countries were encouraged, leading to an economic boom and cultural exchange.

The Lý dynasty ruled until 1225, when it was replaced by the Trần dynasty. Nevertheless, it left a lasting impact on Vietnam's history and identity. Her era is seen as the pinnacle of Vietnamese culture and political stability, which has significantly shaped the country on the path to further development and the preservation of its independence.

The Tran and Hồ Dynasties

The Tran and Hồ dynasties were two important periods in Vietnam's history, which shaped the country through significant political and cultural developments. The Tran Dynasty was founded in 1225 and ruled over Vietnam until 1400. It followed the Lý dynasty and continued its legacy by consolidating Vietnam's stability and territorial influence. Under Tran rule, Vietnam experienced a period of consolidation, strengthening central government and expanding the country further south.

The Tran Dynasty was known for its successful defense against the Mongol invasions under Kublai Khan in the 13th century. The Battle of Bạch Đằng in 1288, where the Vietnamese navy played a decisive role, is considered one of the great military victories in Vietnamese history and cemented the country's independence.

Culturally, the Tran era was characterized by the promotion of education and art. Vietnamese literature flourished, with well-known works such as the national epic "The Legend of Kieu" by Nguyễn Du, which is still considered a masterpiece of Vietnamese literature today. Architectural masterpieces such as the fortress of Đại Việt and the temple complex of Trần Hưng Đạo contributed to the cultural splendor of the time.

The Tran Dynasty was eventually succeeded by the Hồ Dynasty, which ruled from 1400 to 1407. The Hồ Dynasty was short-lived, but marked another phase in Vietnamese history in which the country was destabilized by internal unrest and external threats. During their brief reign, important cultural and political developments continued, but the dynasty was eventually overthrown by the Trần lords.

The Tran and Hồ dynasties together left a significant cultural and historical impact on Vietnam. Their rulers represented times of stability and prosperity, as well as challenges and crises that shaped the country and further cemented its identity as a nation in its own right. Their legacy is highly valued in Vietnamese history and remains an integral part of the country's collective memory.

The Le Dynasty and the Era of the Nguyen Lords

The Le Dynasty and the Nguyen Lords era are two significant periods in Vietnam's history that shaped the country during the late Middle Ages and early modern times. The Le Dynasty was founded in 1428 after successfully defeating the Chinese Ming Dynasty, which had previously occupied Vietnam. The dynasty was led by Lê Lợi, who is revered as a national hero and led Vietnam to independence from Chinese domination.

During the Le Dynasty, Vietnam experienced a period of territorial consolidation and political stability. The central government was strengthened, and important reforms were introduced to govern the country and boost the economy. The Lê rule was also a time of cultural flourishing in which Vietnamese literature, art and architecture were able to flourish. Temples, palaces and literary works were created that are still considered important cultural heirlooms of Vietnam today.

The era of the Nguyen Lords began in the 16th century and was marked by the rule of local Vietnamese lords known as Nguyen. During this time, Vietnam was divided into three regions: the North, Central Vietnam and the South. The Nguyen Lords ruled over these territories, with each lord ruling over a particular region of the country and exercising his own administrative and military controls.

The Nguyen Lords often fought among themselves for power and territory, which led to periods of internal unrest and conflict. Despite these internal disputes, however, the Nguyen Lords managed to maintain their rule over Vietnam until the middle of the 18th century. During this time, important cities such as Huế, the capital of central Vietnam, were developed into centers of culture and political power.

The Nguyen Lords also played a crucial role in Vietnam's diplomatic relations with foreign powers, especially China and Western colonial powers. The Nguyen rulers sought to maintain an act of balance between these powers in order to secure Vietnam's independence while reaping economic benefits from international trade.

The Le Dynasty and the era of the Nguyen Lords were times of change and challenges for Vietnam. While the Le Dynasty united the country and led to a cultural flourishing, the Nguyen Lords' period marked a period of regional rule and geopolitical tensions. Their governments left a lasting influence on Vietnam's development and laid the foundation for the country's later political and social developments into the modern era.

French colonial rule

French colonial rule marked a crucial turning point in Vietnam's history, shaping the country for over a century until the mid-20th century. French expansion in Vietnam began in the 19th century in response to economic interests and the desire to establish a colonial empire in Southeast Asia. The process began slowly, but gained momentum as the French began to expand their presence in Vietnam and establish strategic bases.

The beginning of French colonization can be traced back to the Treaty of Saigon in 1862, through which the French controlled important southern areas of Vietnam. Later, in 1887, the French established the colony of French Indochina, which included Vietnam, Laos, Cambodia and parts of Thailand. This colony served as an economic center for the French exploitation of natural resources and as a military outpost in the region.

During French rule, Vietnam experienced profound social and economic changes. The French invested in infrastructure projects such as the expansion of railway lines, roads and ports, which helped to promote trade and improve transport routes. At the same time, modern administrative structures based on the

French model were introduced, centralising political power.

However, economic development was strongly oriented towards the interests of the French colonial rulers. The indigenous Vietnamese population was often excluded from economic progress and had to endure difficult working conditions in plantations and mines operated by French companies. This led to growing resentment and discontent among the Vietnamese population, which increasingly rebelled against colonial oppression.

Politically, Vietnam was in a situation of dependence during French rule. The French controlled the government through their own officials and a caste of local collaborators, who often ruled against the will of the Vietnamese people. Resistance movements such as the one led by Phan Bội Châu developed to defend Vietnam's independence and challenge French colonial rule.

French colonial rule finally ended after World War II, when the Japanese occupation of Vietnam accelerated the weakening of French control over the country. This led to growing national resistance among Vietnamese nationalists such as Ho Chi Minh, who proclaimed Vietnam's declaration of independence and marked the beginning of the Indochina War against the French colonial power.

The era of French colonial rule was a time of resistance and oppression that left a strong mark on Vietnam. Their impact on the political, economic and social structure of the country was profound and is still present in Vietnam's collective memory and identity today.

The Vietnamese resistance against the colonial power

The Vietnamese resistance to the colonial power was a protracted and determined movement directed against the oppression and exploitation of French colonial rule. From the early stages of French expansion in the 19th century to the country's liberation after World War II, the resistance manifested itself in a variety of ways and through different groups within Vietnamese society.

Even in the early stages of French colonization, signs of resistance were evident. Local leaders and rulers, deposed by the French or seeing their power threatened, organized smaller uprisings and local rebellions. However, these early acts of resistance were often localized and uncoordinated.

Over time, the resistance developed into a national movement, led by intellectual thinkers and revolutionary leaders. Phan Bội Châu, one of the most prominent figures in the Vietnamese resistance, tried to develop a coordinated strategy to regain independence and sought support from other Asian nations.

Resistance grew stronger as Vietnamese nationalists and patriots organized to oppose French colonial rule. An important figure of this time was Hồ Chí Minh, who founded the Communist Party of Vietnam and played a central role in the struggle against the French colonial power. His call for national unity and the liberation of Vietnam from foreign oppression was very popular with the population.

Resistance to the French included a variety of tactics, including political agitation, military action, guerrilla warfare, and diplomatic efforts. The Battle of Điện Biên Phủ in 1954, in which the Viet Minh led by Hồ Chí Minh won a decisive battle against the French army, marked a turning point in the Indochina War and ultimately forced the French to give up their colonial rule.

The decolonization of Vietnam led to the division of the country into North and South Vietnam, with the North under communist leadership and the South under a pro-Western government. Resistance to foreign influences and the aspirations for national unity continued, which eventually led to the Vietnam War and another phase of the struggle for independence and sovereignty of Vietnam.

The Vietnamese resistance against the colonial power was not only a struggle for political freedom, but also for national identity and self-determination. Its impact is deeply rooted in Vietnam's history and memory and has significantly shaped the country on its way to becoming a distinct and united nation.

The Partition of Vietnam: The Vietnam War

The Partition of Vietnam and the Vietnam War represent one of the most turbulent periods in the country's modern history. After the French defeat at Điện Biên Phủ in 1954, Vietnam was divided into two parts: the communist-ruled north and the pro-western south. This division was the result of the Geneva Agreement, which sought a peaceful solution to the conflict between North Vietnam, supported by the Soviet Union and China, and South Vietnam, supported by the United States and Western allies.

The Vietnam War officially began in the late 1950s, when the communist Viet Cong fought in the south against the government of President Ngo Dinh Diem. The United States saw the conflict as part of the Cold War and as a test case for its policy of containing communism in Southeast Asia. The United States began to provide military support to South Vietnam and sent troops to intensify the fight against the Viet Cong and the North Vietnamese forces.

The Vietnam War was characterized by guerrilla warfare and the use of modern war technologies. The United States carried out massive air strikes to disrupt the supply routes and supply lines of the North Vietnamese army. At the same time, the Viet Cong waged a successful guerrilla campaign in the south, attacking both military and civilian targets of the South Vietnamese government and its American allies.

The war led to heavy losses on both sides and caused a humanitarian crisis in the country. U.S. troops peaked in the late 1960s, when more than 500,000 American troops were stationed in Vietnam. However, the war effort was increasingly accompanied by public protests in the United States and around the world that questioned the cost of the war and the moral justification of American intervention.

The Tet Offensive of 1968, the surprise attacks by the Viet Cong on cities and military bases in the south, marked a turning point in the Vietnam War. Although the Tet Offensive was militarily repulsed by the United States and South Vietnam, it showed political leaders in Washington and the world that the war was at an impasse and that the prospects of victory were doubtful.

Negotiations to end the Vietnam War began in the early 1970s and eventually led to the

Paris Agreement of 1973. This agreement provided for the withdrawal of US troops from Vietnam and established a ceasefire between North and South Vietnam. However, the war did not end completely, as the conflict between North and South Vietnam flared up again shortly after the withdrawal of US troops.

In 1975, North Vietnam finally conquered Saigon, the capital of the South, and united the country under communist rule. This marked the end of the Vietnam War and the reunification of Vietnam under one government. The war left deep wounds in Vietnamese society and an enormous burden on the country's economic and social development.

The Vietnam War also had far-reaching implications for international politics and the perception of the United States as a global actor. He became a symbol of resistance to Western intervention and shaped American foreign policy for decades. In Vietnam itself, the war is still a central theme in the collective memory and has shaped the country's national identity and self-perception.

Reunification and the Socialist Republic of Vietnam

The reunification of Vietnam and the establishment of the Socialist Republic of Vietnam marked a decisive phase in the country's history after the end of the Vietnam War. After the conquest of Saigon by North Vietnamese troops in 1975, Vietnam was united under a communist government. The South Vietnamese leadership and numerous civilians fled the communist takeover, which led to major social and political upheavals.

The Socialist Republic of Vietnam was officially proclaimed on July 2, 1976, when the North Vietnamese Hồ Chí Minh, already revered as the father of the nation, was posthumously appointed president. The government pursued a communist ideology based on Marxist-Leninist principles and aimed at the establishment of a socialist state. Politically, parties outside the Communist Party were suppressed, and power was in the hands of the single party, the Communist Party of Vietnam (CP Vietnam).

Economically, Vietnam was confronted with major challenges after reunification. The country had to cope with a destroyed infrastructure, a weakened economy and high social costs of the war. The government relied on a policy of economic reform known as Đổi Mới, which aimed to open up Vietnam and introduce a market economy while maintaining political control.

The Đổi Mới reforms began in the late 1980s under the leadership of Đỗ Mười and Nguyễn Văn Linh and led to a liberalization of the economy, an opening to foreign investment, and a diversification of economic activities. Agricultural reforms have been introduced to increase production, and industrial development programs have been launched to modernize the country's manufacturing base.

Despite economic progress, Vietnam remained a one-party socialist state in which political dissidence and freedom of expression were severely restricted. The CP Vietnam retained political power and controlled all aspects of political life and state institutions. Despite this, Vietnam emerged as one of the fastest-growing economies in Southeast Asia, attracting significant foreign investment, particularly in textiles, electronics and manufacturing.

Over the years, Vietnam has undergone a remarkable transformation, from a war-torn country to an emerging economic power in the region. Social indicators improved significantly, including life expectancy, literacy rates, and access to education and healthcare. Vietnam is now a member of international organizations such as the United Nations, ASEAN and the World Trade Organization (WTO), and plays an increasingly active role in global diplomacy and business.

Reunification and the establishment of the Socialist Republic of Vietnam have shaped the country and shaped its future. Despite challenges, Vietnam remains a country in transition, striving to consolidate its place in the global economy and promote the well-being of its people.

Political system and current developments

Vietnam's political system is characterized by one-party rule by the Communist Party of Vietnam (CP Vietnam), which has been in power since the country's reunification in 1976. The CCP Vietnam is the only legal political party in the country and controls all aspects of government and legislation. The party follows a Marxist-Leninist ideological concept and strives for the establishment of a socialist state based on collectivist principles.

The political system of Vietnam is hierarchically organized, with the top of power being the headquarters of the Politburo of the Communist Party of Vietnam. The Politburo consists of leading party members who determine the political direction of the country and decide on essential political, economic and social issues. The General Secretary of the CP Vietnam, elected by the Politburo, is the country's supreme leader and plays a crucial role in setting the political agenda.

Although there is nominally a legislative National Assembly, elected every five years, this assembly has limited power and is dominated by the Communist Party of

Vietnam. The National Assembly functions more as a political body that formalizes and approves political decisions of the party. The real power lies with the political institutions of the Communist Party of Vietnam, which integrate the executive and legislative functions.

Vietnam has carried out economic reforms in recent decades, known as Đổi Mới, which have led to a liberalization of the economy. These reforms have led to an increase in living standards and an opening to foreign investment, while the political control of the CCP Vietnam has remained largely intact. Despite economic modernization, the political system remains highly centralized and authoritarian, with limited opportunities for political opposition and independent civil society organizations.

In recent years, Vietnam has taken an increasingly active role in international diplomacy by engaging in regional organizations such as ASEAN and global forums. The country has also concluded trade agreements with various countries and regional organizations to promote its economic integration and strengthen its strategic position in the global economy.

Vietnam's political landscape remains dynamic and subject to constant changes influenced by economic development, social mobilization and international relations. The CP Vietnam has sought to strike a balance between economic openness and political stability, seeking to maintain its political control while meeting the growing economic and social needs of the population.

The current developments in Vietnam's political system show an increasing challenge in how the government responds to demands for more political freedom and reforms. The role of the CP Vietnam and its ability to adapt to changing social and political realities will be crucial for the future of the country and its position in the global arena.

Economy and trade in Vietnam

Vietnam's economy has undergone remarkable development in recent decades and has become one of the most dynamic in Southeast Asia. The country has a long history as an agricultural economy, with rice remaining the most important agricultural product and a significant part of exports. Vietnam is one of the largest rice producers in the world and plays a crucial role in the global agricultural commodities market.

In recent years, however, Vietnam has diversified and industrialized its economy. The Đổi Mới reforms of the late 1980s marked a turning point by ushering in an opening of the economy to foreign investment and a liberalization of trade policy. This led to an increase in foreign direct investment, especially in manufacturing, electronics, textiles and footwear.

Vietnam has benefited from its favorable demographic profile, with a young and growing population supporting an increasingly knowledge-based economy. The country has a growing middle class and an emerging consumer market that is an attractive destination for international companies and investors. Cities such as Ho

Chi Minh City and Hanoi are important economic centers that attract a significant portion of economic growth and investment.

The government of Vietnam has pursued a proactive industrial policy to strengthen the competitiveness of domestic industry and promote technological innovation. This includes the promotion of research and development, as well as the creation of special economic zones and industrial parks to attract foreign investment.

Vietnam's integration into the global economy has been fostered by its membership in international organizations such as ASEAN and the World Trade Organization (WTO). The country has signed trade agreements with many countries, including bilateral agreements with major trading partners such as the United States, the EU, China, and other Asian countries. This has helped Vietnam become one of the most important exporters of electronics, footwear, textiles and agricultural products in the region.

Despite economic progress, Vietnam faces challenges such as infrastructure deficiencies, unequal regional development and environmental problems. The government is striving to address these challenges by investing in infrastructure projects, reforming education and health systems, and introducing sustainable development measures.

The future of Vietnam's economy remains promising as the country continues to benefit from its favorable geographical location, young workforce, and increasing integration into the global supply chain. Pursuing economic reforms and promoting an inclusive growth model will be crucial to securing a sustainable development path and meeting the challenges of the 21st century.

Education and health care

Education and health care are crucial pillars for Vietnam's social development. In recent decades, the country has made significant progress in both areas, although challenges such as regional inequalities and limited resources remain.

Vietnam's education system is characterized by a strong emphasis on basic education that should be accessible to all citizens. The literacy rate is over 94%, which is a significant improvement compared to previous decades. The government has made significant efforts to promote basic education and improve access to schools in rural and remote areas.

Higher education in Vietnam has also expanded, with a variety of universities and colleges offering a wide range of courses. Technical education, especially in areas such as engineering and information technology, is particularly in demand and supports the country's growing industry. Vietnam's education system is increasingly focused on promoting skills needed for a modern knowledge society, while at the same time striving to strengthen the quality of teaching and improve infrastructure. In healthcare, Vietnam has made significant progress in making healthcare more accessible to its citizens. The country has built a network of health facilities ranging from large urban hospitals to rural health centers. The government has introduced programs to combat infectious diseases such as HIV/AIDS, tuberculosis, and malaria, and has significantly increased vaccination rates for children. Nevertheless, the health system faces challenges, including limited resources, unequal distribution of medical professionals, and the need for modernized equipment and infrastructure. The government is working to address these challenges by increasing investment in healthcare, expanding medical education programs, and establishing strategic partnerships with international organizations and donor countries.

The COVID-19 pandemic has highlighted the importance of a resilient health system and reinforced the need to further develop public health capacities. Vietnam has done relatively well during the pandemic by taking early measures to contain the virus and conducting a comprehensive vaccination campaign to protect the population.

In summary, education and health care are essential foundations for Vietnam's future development. The country strives to improve the educational level of its citizens and make healthcare accessible to all, while meeting the challenges of a rapidly evolving economy and a changing global health landscape.

Art & Literature in Vietnam

Vietnam's art and literature have a rich and multifaceted history that is deeply rooted in the country's cultural identity. Vietnam's art tradition spans centuries and reflects the diversity of ethnic groups, regions, and historical influences that have shaped the country.

In traditional Vietnamese art, painting, sculpture and handicrafts are in the foreground. The works of art are often characterized by their elegance, attention to detail and the use of symbols and motifs from nature and daily life. For example, the ceramics from Bat Trang and the silk paintings from Hoi An, which preserve traditional techniques and designs, are famous.

Vietnamese literature also has a long tradition, dating back to oral traditions and later to written records. Classic Vietnamese literature includes works such as the "Truyện Kiều" by Nguyễn Du, an epic poem considered a masterpiece of Vietnamese literature, as well as the poems of the poet Hồ Xuân Hương, known for their satirical and sensual nature.

In the modern context, the Vietnamese art and literature scene has undergone a dynamic development, characterized by a mixture of traditional and contemporary influences. Artists and writers deal with current social, political and cultural issues and use different media and forms of expression to convey their messages.

Over the past few decades, Vietnam has become a hub of contemporary art in Southeast Asia, with galleries and art exhibitions in cities such as Hanoi and Ho Chi Minh City providing a platform for Vietnamese and international artists. Modern Vietnamese art is diverse and includes painting, sculpture, installations, performance art, and new media.

Literary festivals and literary events have also gained prominence, with Vietnamese authors and writers being recognized both locally and internationally. Translations of Vietnamese literary works contribute to global visibility, while Vietnamese artists find exhibitions and recognition on international stages.

The government of Vietnam supports art and culture through government programs, scholarships and the promotion of artistic educational institutions. Nevertheless, challenges such as censorship and state control over artistic expressions remain, which can limit free creative expression.

Overall, art and literature in Vietnam reflect a vibrant and dynamic cultural landscape that is shaped by traditions but also integrates new impulses and innovations. The country's artistic scene contributes to cultural identity and helps establish Vietnam as a major player on the global art stage.

Music and traditional Vietnamese instruments

Music and traditional Vietnamese instruments are an integral part of Vietnam's cultural landscape, which has a rich diversity and a long history. Traditional Vietnamese music is strongly influenced by folk music, which has deep roots in the country's rural communities. One of the most well-known forms is the "Nhạc dân tộc cải biên", which involves a redesign and adaptation of traditional folk music pieces to suit modern musical preferences.

Traditional Vietnamese instruments include a variety of stringed instruments such as the đàn bầu, a one-stringed bamboo guitar, the đàn tranh, a zithera-like arched zither, and the đàn nguyệt, a two-stringed crescent moon lute. These instruments each have their own characteristic sound and are often used in traditional Vietnamese music as well as contemporary compositions.

Vietnamese music often uses pentatonic and modal harmonies, which create melodic and rhythmic complexity. It is often accompanied by stories and legends that are passed down through generations through songs and musical interpretations. Important genres include quan họ, a type of lyrical singing that is often accompanied by a dialogue between male and female singers, and ca trù, a form of chamber music performed by a female singer accompanied by a small ensemble of traditional instruments.

The modern Vietnamese music scene has also evolved, with pop music, rock music, and electronic music becoming increasingly popular, especially among the younger generation. Vietnamese pop stars and bands have gained a growing fan base at home and abroad, often fusing traditional Vietnamese elements with Western musical styles.

The government of Vietnam has made efforts to preserve and promote traditional Vietnamese music and instruments by supporting music schools, organizing music festivals, and awarding national artist awards. These measures help to strengthen the country's cultural identity and preserve Vietnam's artistic heritage for future generations.

Overall, music and traditional Vietnamese instruments play a central role in Vietnam's cultural life by providing opportunities for expression, preserving cultural traditions, and bridging the past and present. The diversity and complexity of Vietnam's musical landscape reflects the country's rich cultural diversity, making it a significant part of the global musical heritage.

Religions in Vietnam: Buddhism, Catholicism and folk religions

The religions in Vietnam form a multifaceted fabric of beliefs and spiritual traditions that shape the cultural and social landscape of the country. Buddhism is the predominant religion and plays a central role in the lives of the Vietnamese. Historically, Buddhism was introduced to Vietnam in the 2nd century and has since taken deep roots. The majority of the Vietnamese population practices Mahayana Buddhism, especially the lineage of Vietnamese Zen Buddhism, which is known for its emphasis on meditation and enlightenment. Monasteries and pagodas are widespread throughout the country and serve as centers for spiritual practice and community life.

In addition to Buddhism, Catholicism also plays an important role in Vietnam, especially among the ethnic minority of Vietnamese who belong to the Christian faith. The Catholic Church has a long history in Vietnam, dating back to the arrival of Portuguese missionaries in the 16th century. Vietnam is one of the countries with the largest Catholic population in Southeast Asia, and many believers are organized in rural and urban communities closely linked to the Vatican hierarchy.

In addition to Buddhism and Catholicism, many Vietnamese also practice traditional folk religions and ancestor worship. These religions are often associated with local customs, rituals, and beliefs that are deeply rooted in Vietnamese culture. Ancestor worship is a central part of religious life and social structure in Vietnam, with family altars and annual rituals in memory of the deceased playing an important role.

The influence of these religions on the daily lives of Vietnamese people is wide-ranging, from traditional festivals and holidays to social and ethical norms that influence behavior and interpersonal relationships. Despite secularization tendencies in modern society, religiosity remains deeply rooted and continues to shape cultural identity and community ties in Vietnam.

The government of Vietnam officially practices a policy of religious freedom, although it also regulates and controls religious activities. Religious groups must register and comply with certain regulations, which occasionally leads to tensions between state interests and religious communities. Nevertheless, Vietnamese religions have shown remarkable resilience and maintained their presence in the country's public life, highlighting their diversity and influence in a changing society.

Daily life in Vietnam

Daily life in Vietnam is characterized by a variety of cultural traditions, economic dynamism and social diversity. Urban centres such as Hanoi and Ho Chi Minh City are bustling with activity, characterised by a mix of traditional markets and modern shopping centres. The street life is vibrant and vibrant, with an abundance of motorbikes, bicycles and pedestrians winding through the narrow streets and wide boulevards.

Family plays a central role in the daily life of the Vietnamese, with a strong emphasis on traditional values such as respect for the elders and solidarity within the family. Multi-generational houses are common, in which several generations live under one roof and work together to ensure the well-being of the family. This close family bond often extends beyond relatives to close friends and neighbors who meet regularly in community gardens or temples to strengthen social bonds and celebrate shared traditions.

Vietnamese cuisine is another central part of daily life, with fresh ingredients such as herbs, vegetables, fish and rice forming the basis of many dishes. Pho, a hearty noodle soup, is perhaps the most well-known

Vietnamese dish to enjoy at any time of the day. Eating is often a social event where family members and friends come together to cook and eat together.

The education system in Vietnam is strongly focused on achievement and success, with education seen as the key to personal and professional success. Students often undergo extra hours of tutoring courses to maximize their chances of a successful future. Higher education is highly valued, and competition for places in the best universities is intense.

In rural areas of Vietnam, many people continue traditional ways of life that are closely linked to agriculture. Rice fields dominate the landscape, and farmers often use traditional methods to grow and harvest their crops. Village communities maintain close relationships and regularly celebrate festivals and ceremonies dedicated to the seasons and harvest successes.

The health system in Vietnam has improved, but many people still have limited access to medical care, especially in rural areas. The government is striving to expand health care and improve the quality of life of citizens by building health centers and implementing public health programs.

Daily life in Vietnam is characterized by a dynamic mix of tradition and modernity, which is reflected in the country's architecture, cuisine, culture and social structures. As Vietnam continues to develop and strengthen its role in the global economy, the cultural roots and community spirit of the Vietnamese remain strong and alive.

Traditional clothing and fashion

Vietnam's traditional clothing and fashion reflect a rich cultural history and the diversity of ethnic groups that inhabit the country. One of the most well-known forms of traditional Vietnamese clothing is the Ao Dai, an elegant, figure-hugging garment worn by both men and women. The Ao Dai consists of a long, tight-fitting tunic over a pair of wide trousers and is often worn on special occasions such as weddings, celebrations and national festivals.

Ethnic minorities in Vietnam also wear their own traditional clothing styles, often rich in colors, embroideries and specific patterns that express the cultural identity and origin of the wearers. Examples of this are the colorful robes of the Hmong, the elaborately embroidered costumes of the Dao or the finely woven textiles of the Cham.

In addition to traditional clothing, the modern Vietnamese fashion industry has also developed, especially in cities such as Hanoi and Ho Chi Minh City, where designers and fashion design schools support emerging talent. Vietnamese designers often combine traditional craft techniques with modern cuts and materials to create innovative collections that attract local and international attention.

The use of silk, cotton and linen is widespread in Vietnamese fashion, with each material having its own characteristics and cultural meanings. Silk, known for its softness and luster, is often used for formal ao dai and festive occasions, while cotton and linen are preferred for everyday use and workwear.

Traditional crafts play an important role in the production of Vietnamese clothing and fashion accessories. Hand-embroidered bags, scarves and hats are popular souvenirs for tourists and a sign of the high craftsmanship of Vietnamese craftsmen. The preservation and promotion of these crafts is an important part of efforts to preserve and pass on Vietnam's cultural heritage.

In recent years, Vietnam has also established itself as a production hub for the global fashion industry, with many international brands having their clothes made in Vietnamese factories. This development has brought both economic opportunities and challenges, including questions about working conditions and the environmental impact of fashion production.

Overall, Vietnam's traditional clothing and fashion reflects a fascinating mix of cultural tradition, craftsmanship, and modern design. It is not only an expression of personal identity, but also a window into the country's rich cultural landscape, which inspires and fascinates visitors and locals alike.

Vietnamese cuisine: flavours and influences

Vietnamese cuisine is famous for its fresh flavors, diverse flavors, and healthy ingredients that reflect a rich culinary tradition. It combines influences from different regions of Vietnam as well as from Chinese, French and Thai cuisine. The basis of many Vietnamese dishes is rice and rice products, which play a central role in the country's culture and are used in various forms such as rice noodles, rice paper and rice rolls.

One of the most famous and popular Vietnamese foods is pho, a hearty noodle soup with beef or chicken served with fresh herbs, limes, chili, and soy sauce. In addition to being a symbol of Vietnamese cuisine, this soup is an integral part of the daily lives of many Vietnamese, who enjoy it for both breakfast and dinner.

Another signature dish is the banh mi, a French-Vietnamese sandwich consisting of a crispy baguette filled with various ingredients such as marinated meat, pickled vegetables, fresh herbs and mayonnaise. Banh Mi is a popular snack or quick meal that can be found at street stalls and small takeaways across the country.

Fish and seafood play an important role in Vietnamese cuisine, as Vietnam has a long coastline and many rivers and lakes are rich in fish. Popular dishes include cha ca, fried fish with turmeric and dill, as well as various types of grilled or steamed fish, often served with rice and vegetables.

Vietnamese cuisine is known for its balanced diet and the use of fresh ingredients such as herbs, vegetables, fresh fruits and spices such as lemongrass, mint and coriander. These ingredients not only add flavor to the dishes, but also contribute to their healthy and nutritious quality.

In addition to savory dishes, Vietnam also has a variety of sweets and desserts, often based on rice, coconut milk, fruits and beans. Examples include Che, a sweet rice pudding with various toppings such as coconut milk, fruits, and jelly-like pearls, and Banh Xeo, crispy rice pancakes filled with shrimp, pork, and bean sprouts.

Vietnamese food culture is also heavily influenced by traditional eating habits, such as eating together in large groups and sharing dishes at the dinner table. Meals are often social occasions where family and friends come together to enjoy and celebrate their love of Vietnamese cuisine.

In recent years, Vietnamese cuisine has gained international recognition, with Vietnamese restaurants and street food stalls being popular worldwide. The variety of flavors and the freshness of the ingredients make Vietnamese cuisine one of the most exciting and eclectic culinary traditions in Asia, appealing to both palates and senses alike.

National dishes of Vietnam

Vietnam's national dishes are a reflection of the country's rich culinary traditions and diversity, which offers a wealth of tastes and ingredients from north to south and east to west. Among the outstanding national dishes of Vietnam, pho is certainly the most famous and popular. This hearty noodle soup is made with a clear broth, rice noodles, tender beef or chicken, and a variety of fresh herbs such as cilantro, Thai basil, and mint. Pho is an integral part of Vietnamese food, both as breakfast and as a snack or dinner.

Another prominent national dish is bun cha, especially popular in Hanoi. It consists of grilled pork served in a sweet and sour broth, along with rice noodles, fresh salad and herbs. Bun Cha is known for its combination of savory meat flavor and the freshness of the accompanying ingredients that make it a treat for the senses.

Goi Cuon, fresh summer rolls, are also an icon of Vietnamese cuisine and are made from thin rice paper rolls filled with shrimp, pork, rice noodles and fresh vegetables such as lettuce, cucumbers and herbs. Often served with a sweet and spicy peanut sauce, they are a light and healthy choice for a meal or snack. Com Tam, broken rice, is another popular national dish that is often sold as a street food throughout Vietnam. It consists of shredded broken rice served with grilled pork, a fried egg, salad and pickled vegetables. Com Tam is known for its ease of preparation and savory flavor that makes it a favorite among locals.

For seafood lovers, Ca Kho To, braised fish in caramel sauce, is a must. This dish is made with fresh fish that is slowly cooked in a mixture of caramel, fish sauce, garlic and spices until it is tender and aromatic. Often served with rice, Ca Kho To exemplifies the refined balance of sweet, salty, and spicy that characterizes Vietnamese cuisine.

In addition to these main dishes, there are a variety of side dishes, snacks, and street food that enrich Vietnam's food culture. Banh Xeo, crispy rice pancakes filled with shrimp, pork and bean sprouts, as well as Banh Mi, a French-Vietnamese baguette sandwich with marinated meat, pickled vegetables and fresh herbs, are just a few examples of the diversity and sense of taste of Vietnamese cuisine.

Vietnam's national dishes reflect not only the country's culinary creativity and diversity, but also its history, culture, and connection to nature and the seasons. From the green rice fields of the north to the lush river deltas of the south, Vietnam offers a wealth of tastes that inspire and delight visitors and locals alike.

Street food and local delicacies

Street food and local delicacies are an integral part of Vietnam's food culture, offering a variety of delicious and affordable options for locals and visitors alike. The streets of Hanoi, Ho Chi Minh City, and many other towns and villages across the country are home to an abundance of stalls and food stalls offering a variety of dishes, often freshly prepared and served in front of customers.

Pho, one of the most famous Vietnamese specialties, is offered as a quick meal not only in restaurants but also on the street stalls. The steaming noodle soup with tender beef or chicken, fresh herbs, and limes is a favorite among locals, especially for breakfast or as a snack between meals.

Banh Mi, the Vietnamese sandwich, is another popular street food that can be found in bakeries and small food stalls. The crispy baguette is served with a variety of fillings such as marinated meat (usually pork), pickled vegetables, fresh herbs and a spicy sauce. Banh Mi is not only tasty, but also an inexpensive and convenient food to eat on the go.

Goi cuon, fresh summer rolls, are another characteristic street food of Vietnam. These light and healthy rolls are made from thin sheets of rice paper and served with shrimp, pork, rice noodles, fresh herbs, and often a touch of garlic as well. They are served with a sweet and spicy dipping sauce made with fish sauce, lime juice, sugar and chili oil and are especially popular during the hot summer months.

In addition to these well-known dishes, the street stalls also offer a variety of local specialties, which can vary depending on the region. For example, Bun Thit Nuong, grilled pork noodles with vegetables and peanuts, are popular in central Vietnam, while Banh Xeo, crispy rice pancakes filled with shrimp, pork and bean sprouts, are especially found in the south of the country.

The variety and quality of Vietnamese street food is a testament to people's love of good food and a rich culinary tradition that has lasted for generations. The street stalls not only offer inexpensive meals, but are also a social gathering place where locals come together to exchange ideas and enjoy their favorite foods. Street food in Vietnam is not only a way to get to know the local cuisine, but also an experience for the senses that attracts and delights visitors from all over the world.

Vietnam's wildlife: from the red river dolphin to the Javan rhinoceros

Vietnam's wildlife is characterized by an amazing diversity and is home to many unique species that live in the country's different ecosystems. One of Vietnam's iconic animal species is the red river dolphin, also known as the Tonkin dolphin, which can be found in the Mekong Delta and other rivers in the north of the country. These rare freshwater dolphins are highly endangered and under strict protection as their populations have declined sharply due to habitat loss and fishing activities.

Vietnam's dense forests are home to various primate species, including the black langur and the white-shanked gibbon. These monkey species are known for their ability to adapt to the treetops and play an important role in the ecological balance of the rainforests by acting as seed dispersers and contributing to the diversity of plants.

The Javan hornbill, also known as the Great Hornbill, is an imposing bird found in the tropical forests of Vietnam. With its distinctive yellow and black plumage and massive beak, the Javan hornbill is a symbol of the biodiversity of the Asian rainforests. These birds play an important ecological role by serving as seed dispersers for a variety of tree species and contributing to the biodiversity of the region through their presence.

Vietnam is also home to a variety of reptiles and amphibians, including the green sea turtle, which is found on the country's coasts and waters. This endangered turtle species comes to the coasts of Vietnam to lay its eggs and is under protective measures due to habitat loss, illegal fishing and pollution.

The waters around Vietnam are home to numerous marine life, including the dugong, also known as the manatee, as well as various shark species such as the whale shark, the largest fish in the world's oceans. These marine species are crucial to the ecological balance of marine ecosystems and are protected to conserve their stock.

Vietnam's wildlife also includes an abundance of insect species, including butterflies, beetles, and dragonflies that live in the country's tropical forests and wetlands. Many of these insect species are crucial for the pollination of plants and play an important role in the food web of ecosystems.

Overall, Vietnam's wildlife is a natural treasure that must be preserved through the protection and sustainable use of the country's natural resources. The diversity of species and the ecological importance of Vietnam's wildlife make it a significant draw for nature lovers, researchers, and environmentalists from around the world who visit the country to experience and protect its unique biodiversity.

Nature conservation and environmental problems

Vietnam's conservation and environmental issues are at the heart of an ongoing debate and efforts to preserve the country's rich biodiversity and minimize environmental impact. Vietnam is rich in diverse ecosystems, including tropical rainforests, coastal and marine areas, and river deltas that provide a variety of habitats for an enormous variety of plant and animal species. However, these ecosystems are increasingly threatened by human activities, including deforestation, poaching, overfishing, and pollution.

Deforestation is one of Vietnam's biggest environmental problems. Despite efforts to achieve sustainable forest management, deforestation remains a serious threat to the country's natural habitats. Tropical rainforests are particularly affected, as they not only serve as home to many endemic species, but also help regulate the climate and maintain soil fertility.

Poaching is another critical issue that endangers Vietnam's wildlife. Many animal species, including elephants, rhinos, tigers, and various primates, are illegally hunted or captured to sell their body parts for the black market. Despite strict protective measures, poaching activities continue to be a threat to the country's biodiversity.

Overfishing and pollution of marine and coastal areas are serious challenges for Vietnam's marine environment. With over 3,000 kilometers of coastline, Vietnam is heavily dependent on fishing, but overfishing leads to depletion of fish stocks and threatens the long-term sustainability of the fishing industry. In addition, the marine environment suffers from the effects of industrial pollution, waste management and oil pollution, which endanger both marine fauna and coastal ecosystems.

Air pollution is a growing problem, especially in urban areas such as Hanoi and Ho Chi Minh City. Increasing vehicle traffic and industrial activities contribute to air pollution, which leads to health problems for the urban population and affects the overall quality of the environment.

Despite these challenges, Vietnam is making considerable efforts in the field of nature conservation and environmental preservation. The country has established numerous national parks and nature reserves to protect endangered species and preserve natural habitats. International cooperation and support also play an important role in tackling global environmental problems such as climate change and sustainable development.

Overall, Vietnam faces complex environmental problems that challenge the sustainable development of the country. Through ongoing efforts for nature conservation, sustainable resource use and environmental education, Vietnam strives to protect its unique biodiversity and leave a healthy and livable environment for future generations.

Hanoi: capital and cultural center

Hanoi, the capital of Vietnam, is not only the political and administrative center of the country, but also an important cultural and historical center. The city, which stretches along the banks of the Red River, has a rich history that dates back to 1010, when it was named the capital of the country by King Ly Thai To. Since then, Hanoi has played a key role in Vietnam's development and has become a significant cultural hub in Southeast Asia.

One of Hanoi's most distinctive features is its architecture, which is a testament to its chequered history. The Old Town, known as the "36 Street District", is made up of a maze of narrow streets and colonial buildings from the French colonial era. It is also home to numerous Buddhist temples, pagodas, and historic buildings that reflect the cultural diversity of the city.

Hoan Kiem Lake, a central point in Hanoi, is a popular meeting place for locals and tourists alike. Surrounded by parks and historical monuments, the lake is known for its idyllic beauty and the legends that revolve around the giant turtle that is said to live in the water.

Culturally, Hanoi offers a rich palette of art, literature and traditional music. The Vietnam National Museum of History, the Vietnam Museum of Fine Arts, and the Hanoi Temple of Literature are just a few of the cultural sites that offer insight into Vietnam's rich history and culture. The city is also known for its vibrant art scene, with numerous galleries, theaters, and venues for traditional Vietnamese music and dance.

Hanoi is also a major educational center with several prestigious universities and educational institutions. The city attracts young people from all over the country who study here and specialize in various academic disciplines.

As the political center of the country, Hanoi is home to important government buildings and diplomatic missions. The Presidential Palace, the headquarters of the Communist Party of Vietnam and the Ho Chi Minh Mausoleum are important symbols of the country's political power and history.

In recent decades, Hanoi has experienced remarkable economic development and has become an important commercial and economic center. The city is home to numerous industries, including electronics, textiles, and tourism, which contribute to Vietnam's economic dynamism.

Hanoi remains a fascinating city that captivates its visitors with its historical depth, cultural richness and dynamic atmosphere. As the capital and cultural center of Vietnam, Hanoi plays a key role in the country's national identity and will continue to play a significant role in the Southeast Asia region.

Ho Chi Minh City (Saigon): Economic heart of Vietnam

Ho Chi Minh City, formerly known as Saigon, is the economic heart of Vietnam and one of the most dynamic cities in Southeast Asia. Named after the national leader Ho Chi Minh, the city is the economic center of the country and plays a crucial role in the industrial and commercial sectors. With a population of over 9 million people, Ho Chi Minh City is also the largest city in Vietnam and a major hub for trade, education, and culture.

The city is famous for its modern architecture, bustling markets, and vibrant streets. The contrast between historic colonial buildings from the French colonial era and ultra-modern skyscrapers reflects the rapid development that Ho Chi Minh City has experienced in recent decades. As an important commercial and industrial hub, the city attracts investors from all over the world and is home to numerous international companies as well as Vietnamese conglomerates.

Ho Chi Minh City's economic growth is driven by various sectors, including manufacturing, technology, services, and tourism. The city is a leading center for the production of electronics, textiles, food, and other consumer goods. The proximity to major ports such as Cat Lai Port and Tan Son Nhat International Airport supports trade and logistics, which contributes to the economic dynamism of the region.

Educational institutions such as Ho Chi Minh University and the University of Economics and Finance provide a solid academic foundation for the city's young population. Ho Chi Minh City's education system attracts students from all over the country who study here and specialize in various disciplines, further fostering the city's intellectual and cultural diversity.

Culturally, Ho Chi Minh City is rich in history and traditions. Museums such as the War Remnants Museum and the History Museum offer insights into Vietnam's chequered past, especially during the Vietnam War and the French colonial period. The city is also known for its vibrant art scene, with numerous galleries, theaters, and cultural events highlighting the creative potential of Vietnamese artists.

The people of Ho Chi Minh City are known for their hospitality and enterprising. The street markets such as Ben Thanh Market are not only places of trade, but also social meeting places where visitors can taste the local cuisine and gain insights into the everyday life of the city's inhabitants.

In recent years, Ho Chi Minh City has experienced impressive urban development, which is reflected in the modernization of infrastructure and the improvement of the quality of life of residents. Despite challenges such as traffic congestion and pollution, the city remains a symbol of Vietnam's economic boom and its role as a major player in the global economy.

Ho Chi Minh City, with its mix of history, culture and economic vitality, remains a fascinating destination for visitors and a dynamic home for its inhabitants. As the economic heart of Vietnam, the city will continue to play a key role in the country's development and serve as a major center for trade, education, and innovation in the Southeast Asia region.

Huế: The Imperial City on the Perfume River

Huế, the former imperial capital of Vietnam, is picturesquely located on the banks of the Perfume River and is an important cultural and historical center of the country. The city was founded in 1802 by Emperor Gia Long as the capital of the Nguyen Empire and remained the political center of Vietnam under the Nguyen rulers until 1945. Hue is known for its magnificent architecture, which is influenced by traditional Vietnamese aesthetics and imperial rule.

One of the most outstanding sights in Huế is the Imperial City, a massive fortress complex with palatial structures, temples, courtyards and administrative buildings. The imperial city, also known as the Citadel of Huế, covers an area of over 500 hectares and is surrounded by an imposing wall that once protected the political and cultural center of the Nguyen Empire. Within the Imperial City are several significant buildings, including the Purple Forbidden City, the Ngo Mon Archway, and the Hall of Supreme Harmony, which served imperial and state ceremonies.

In addition to being an imperial city, Hue is also known for its multitude of historic temples and pagodas that stretch across the city and its surrounding hills. The Thien Mu Pagoda, a seven-story pagoda on the banks of the Perfume River, is considered the symbol of Huê and is home to a number of Buddhist statues and relics. The scent of the perfume river that flows through the city adds to the picturesque atmosphere and is a popular backdrop for tourists and photographers.

Culturally, Huế is also known for its traditional Vietnamese music, especially the court music of the Nguyen dynasty. This form of music, known as Nhã Nhạc, has been declared an Intangible Cultural Heritage of Humanity by UNESCO and is still performed today in Huế and other parts of Vietnam. The city is also known for its culinary specialties, including the famous dish Bun Bo Huế, a spicy noodle soup with beef that originated in the region.

Huế played a significant role during the Vietnam War and was the scene of several battles and strategic operations. Although many historic buildings and monuments were damaged during the war, the city has still preserved and restored much of its cultural heritage.

Today, Huế is a major tourist attraction and a center for education and culture in central Vietnam. Home to several universities and research institutions, the city attracts both national and international visitors who want to explore the rich history, architecture, and culture of the former imperial city.

Huế, with its unique blend of imperial heritage, scenic beauty, and cultural significance, remains one of Vietnam's most fascinating cities and a symbol of the country's rich history and tradition.

Hội An: The Historic Trade Center

Hội An, a charming city on Vietnam's central coast, is a jewel of history and trade. Originally founded as a port city, Hoi An experienced its heyday during the Vietnamese Nguyen Dynasty in the 16th and 17th centuries. The city developed into an important trading center, called the Silk Road of the Sea, and was an important hub for trade between East and West.

The architecture of Hoi An is unique and reflects its multicultural past. Hoi An's Old Town is a UNESCO World Heritage Site and features well-preserved buildings from the Japanese, Chinese, Vietnamese, and French colonial periods. The characteristic yellow buildings with red-tiled roofs and decorative wood carvings give the town a quaint charm that attracts visitors from all over the world.

A prominent feature of Hoi An are the old trading houses that served as meeting places and residences for wealthy merchants. These houses are a living example of the thriving commercial activity and cultural exchange that took place in the city. The most famous among them is the Tan Ky House, which has been inhabited by the same family for several generations and has retained its original architecture and furnishings.

Hoi An was an important transshipment point for silk, spices, ceramics and other valuable goods traded by traders from China, Japan, India and Europe. The city's history is also reflected in its markets, such as the Central Market and the Night Market, where visitors can buy local products and handicrafts.

The cultural diversity of Hoi An is also evident in its religious sites. The city is known for its variety of temples and pagodas, including the Fujian Worship Complex, Chùa Cầu Pagoda (the Japanese Bridge), and Quan Cong Pagoda, all of which reflect unique architecture and religious practices.

In addition to its historical heritage, Hoi An is also known for its culinary delights. The local cuisine is rich in flavor and variety, with dishes such as cao lau (a specialty noodle) and white rose (stuffed dumplings) typical of the region. Visitors can also visit traditional Vietnamese coffee houses and enjoy the relaxed atmosphere of the city.

Today, Hội An is not only a tourist center, but also a city that has preserved and developed its historical identity. The preservation of the old town and the promotion of cultural heritage are crucial to preserving the unique character of Hoi An, making it an unforgettable destination for history buffs and lovers of Vietnamese culture.

Dalat: The City of Flowers and Eternal Spring

Dalat, often known as the "City of Flowers" or "City of Eternal Spring", is picturesquely located in the central highlands of Vietnam. Founded by the French in the late 19th century, the city quickly became a popular retreat for its cool temperatures and picturesque scenery. At an altitude of about 1500 meters above sea level, Dalat offers a temperate climate that is very different from the hotter regions of Vietnam.

The city is famous for its lush gardens and flower plantations that are in full bloom all year round. Particularly well-known are the huge dahlia fields and the flower exhibitions that take place regularly and attract visitors from all over the world. Dalat is also a major producer of flowers and offers a variety of plants grown both for the local market and for export.

The architecture of Dalat is equally remarkable, clearly bearing French and colonial influences. Many of the historic buildings and villas in the center of the city are well preserved and reflect the charm of yesteryear. The Dalat Palace Hotel, the Dalat Opera House, and the Con Ga Church are some of the most striking examples of colonial architecture that visitors can admire.

In addition to its natural beauty and architecture, Dalat is also known for its cultural diversity and culinary delights. The city is home to a significant number of ethnic minorities, including the K'ho and Lat people, who have preserved their traditional way of life and cultural customs. Tourists have the opportunity to visit the villages of the ethnic minorities and learn more about their traditions, crafts and way of life.

Dalat is also a paradise for adventure lovers and outdoor enthusiasts. The surrounding mountains and forests offer numerous hiking and trekking opportunities, while Xuan Huong Lake in the center of the city provides an idyllic backdrop for boat trips and picnics. Golf lovers can play on one of the city's picturesque golf courses, which benefit from its natural surroundings and breathtaking views.

The economy of Dalat is mainly based on agriculture and tourism. In addition to growing flowers and vegetables, the city is also known for its coffee plantations, which produce some of the best coffee in Vietnam. Tourism plays an increasingly important role in the local economy, with hotels, restaurants and tour companies catering to the growing number of visitors looking to discover the beauty and charm of Dalat.

Overall, Dalat is a city that fascinates with its unique combination of natural beauty, cultural diversity and historical significance. Its pleasant climatic conditions, coupled with a rich cultural scene and diverse recreational opportunities, make Dalat an unforgettable destination for anyone who wants to experience the authentic Vietnam.

Halong Bay: A UNESCO World Heritage Site

Halong Bay, a UNESCO World Heritage Site, is undoubtedly one of Vietnam's most impressive natural wonders. Located in the Gulf of Tonkin in the north of the country, this picturesque bay covers an area of around 1,500 square kilometers and consists of over 1,600 limestone cliffs and islands rising from the emerald waters. This unique landscape has captured the imagination of travelers and artists for centuries and is one of the most visited tourist attractions in the country.

The limestone cliffs of Halong Bay were formed about 500 million years ago by sediment deposits on the seafloor. Over millions of years, erosion by wind and water formed these spectacular rock formations, which today rise out of the sea like stone sculptures. Some of the rocks have poetic names that resemble their shape, such as the rock "Fighting Cocks" or "Incense Burner".

In addition to the imposing limestone cliffs, Halong Bay is also known for its caves and grottoes, some of which are open to visitors. The most famous among them is the cave of Thien Cung (Sky Grotto), whose extensive chambers are decorated with stalactites and stalagmites that have formed over centuries.

Halong Bay is not only a natural wonder, but also a rich ecosystem that is home to a variety of marine life and birds. The waters are rich in marine life, including numerous species of fish, crabs, shrimp and mussels. Of particular note is the red langur, a rare species of primate that lives in the forests on some of the bay's islands and is a protected species.

The cultural history of Halong Bay goes back a long way and is closely linked to Vietnamese history and mythology. Local legends tell of dragons that once jumped out of the mountains into the sea, leaving behind the islands and rocks that now form the bay. These legends have given the bay its Vietnamese name "Vịnh Hạ Long", which translates to "Bay of the Descending Dragon".

Tourists can explore Halong Bay in a variety of ways, including boat rides on traditional junks or modern cruise ships. The bay also offers opportunities for kayaking, swimming, and diving, allowing visitors to experience the beauty and mysterious atmosphere of this UNESCO World Heritage Site firsthand.

In recent years, tourism has increased in Halong Bay, which poses challenges for the preservation of the environment and ecological balance. Measures to protect the bay and its unique ecosystems are therefore crucial to preserve its beauty and value for future generations.

Halong Bay remains an unparalleled pearl in Vietnam's landscape, captivating visitors with its natural beauty, rich history, and cultural heritage. It is a living testament to the wonders of nature and a source of endless inspiration for travelers from all over the world.

The temple city of My Son

The temple city of My Son is an important archaeological site in central Vietnam, located about 69 kilometers southwest of Da Nang. It includes the remains of a once magnificent religious center of the Cham culture, built between the 4th and 13th centuries AD. My Son is known for its well-preserved temple ruins, which offer a fascinating insight into the religious and artistic traditions of the Cham people.

The history of My Son dates back to the 4th century, when the first Hindu temples were built on the site. The Cham rulers built a large number of temples dedicated to the Hindu deities Shiva, Vishnu, and others. These temples served as religious and cultural centers for the Cham Kingdom, which ruled large parts of central and southern Vietnam in its heyday.

The architecture of My Son is remarkable for its artistic design and symbolic meaning. The temples are built of brick and decorated with stone reliefs, sculptures, and ornate columns that reflect the religious beliefs and myths of the Cham people. The Cham artists created unique works that depict the Hindu cosmos and stories from epic and mythology.

Over the centuries, My Son experienced a period of rise and decline, influenced by political upheaval and armed conflicts in the region. Especially during the 7th to 10th centuries, the temple city experienced a heyday, during which it flourished as a religious and cultural center of the Cham culture. It was a place of prayer, offerings and spiritual pilgrimages for the Cham society.

The discovery and exploration of My Son began in the 19th century by French explorers who recognized the historical significance of the site and began documenting and restoring its ruins. Although My Son has been severely damaged over time by wars, natural disasters and the ravages of time, it remains an important heritage of the Cham culture and a UNESCO World Heritage Site since 1999.

Visitors to My Son will have the opportunity to explore the various temple ruins and discover the rich history and art of the Cham culture. The archaeological complex includes numerous temple platforms, shrines, and towers arranged along a central axis pathway. This trail leads to the most important temples, including the main temple (Kalan) and smaller side shrines that fulfilled a variety of religious functions.

My Son's importance as an archaeological site extends beyond its artistic and religious significance, offering insight into Cham society, its religious practices, and its cultural development over the centuries. The preservation and restoration of the temple ruins remains a challenge and a priority to preserve and explore this unique cultural heritage for future generations.

The Tunnels of Củ Chi

The Củ Chi Tunnels represent a remarkable military infrastructure built and used by Vietnamese guerrilla fighters, the Viet Cong, during the Vietnam War. These tunnels not only served as a hiding place from enemy attacks, but also played a central role in the strategic defense and supply of fighters during the conflict.

The network of Củ Chi Tunnels stretches over an impressive length of several hundred kilometers, although the exact extent can vary depending on the source and the infrastructure preserved. Originally, the construction of the tunnels began in the 1940s during the struggle against French colonial rule and was then further expanded and strengthened during the Vietnam War.

The tunnels were an integral part of the Viet Cong's tactics, which waged asymmetrical warfare against the better-equipped American and South Vietnamese forces. They were used not only as hiding places, but also as communication routes, weapons depots, infirmaries and even as living quarters for the fighters and their families.

The tunnel network of Củ Chi was extremely ingeniously designed. The tunnels themselves were narrow and often only large enough for a person to crawl through them. They were laid out in several levels, sometimes up to three levels deep underground, to protect them from bombing. The entrances to the tunnels were carefully camouflaged, often hidden as inconspicuous openings in the forest or underground.

During the Vietnam War, the tunnels of Củ Chi became a symbol of the resistance and determination of the Vietnamese people in the struggle for independence and national unity. They played a crucial role in numerous military operations, including during the Tet Offensive of 1968, when the Viet Cong launched coordinated attacks throughout South Vietnam.

The Củ Chi Tunnels are now a major tourist attraction in Vietnam, offering visitors a glimpse into the history of the Vietnam War. Some sections of the tunnels have been opened to visitors, with the opportunity to crawl through the narrow passageways and experience the conditions in which the Viet Cong fighters lived and fought during the war.

The preservation of the tunnels of Củ Chi is a challenge due to natural weathering and the increasing number of visitors. Nevertheless, its importance as a historical heritage and symbol of Vietnamese resistance remains undisputed. The Củ Chi Tunnels stand as a monument to the determination and sacrifice of the Vietnamese people in one of the darkest periods of their modern history.

The Mekong Delta Region: Life in the River

The Mekong Delta in Vietnam is a fascinating region characterized by the mighty Mekong River, which meanders through six countries of Southeast Asia and flows into the South China Sea in an extensive delta in Vietnam. The delta covers an area of around 40,000 square kilometres and is known for its fertile soils and the diversity of life forms that are closely linked to the water.

The Mekong River, which originates in Tibet and flows through China, Myanmar, Laos, Thailand and Cambodia, eventually reaches Vietnam and divides into numerous river arms and canals that form the delta. These waterways are not only vital to the region's agriculture and fisheries, but also shape the daily lives of the people who live along the river and its tributaries.

The population in the Mekong Delta is made up of a variety of ethnic groups, including Kinh (Vietnamese) as well as Khmer and various minorities. The people live mainly from agriculture, with rice, fish and fruit being the most important products. The delta's fertile alluvial soils and humid climate support intensive agriculture, which makes the delta one of Vietnam's most productive agricultural regions.

The Mekong Delta is also known for its unique ecosystem diversity. The wetlands, mangrove forests and freshwater ecosystems provide habitat for a variety of animal and plant species, including rare bird species such as the swan goose and the sambar deer. The delta's arms and canals are home to fish such as the giant catfish and avocet, which are an important source of food for the local population.

The traditional way of life in the Mekong Delta is closely linked to water. Many communities live in floating villages or on stilt houses on the banks of the rivers. Water transportation is widespread, and boats are used for trade, transportation of goods, and daily traffic. Riverside markets are vibrant hubs of commerce and social interaction, where locals and visitors alike can pick up fresh produce and handmade goods.

Tourists visiting the Mekong Delta can have a unique cultural experience by visiting traditional villages, interacting with locals, and experiencing traditional handicrafts. Boat trips through the delta offer glimpses of the rich nature and life along the river, including the chance to sample exotic fruits and enjoy local dishes prepared with fresh local ingredients.

However, the challenges of climate change and pollution increasingly pose a threat to the Mekong Delta. Rising sea levels, salinization of soils and deterioration of water quality have an impact on agricultural production and the livelihoods of the population. Nevertheless, the Mekong Delta remains a dynamic and vibrant region that fascinates with its natural beauty, cultural diversity and economic importance.

The beaches of Phú Quốc and Nha Trang

Phú Quốc and Nha Trang are among the most famous beach destinations in Vietnam, attracting thousands of visitors each year who want to enjoy the natural beauty of the coasts and tropical climate. Phú Quốc, the largest island in Vietnam, is located in the Gulf of Thailand off the coast of the Cambodian province of Kep. With its pristine white sand beaches and crystal clear waters, Phú Quốc is a paradise for sun worshippers and water sports enthusiasts alike. The island is known for its laid-back atmosphere and the variety of resort hotels that stretch along the coast, offering a wide range of accommodation, from luxury boutique resorts to affordable guesthouses.

Nha Trang, on the other hand, is located on the central coast of Vietnam on the South China Sea and is famous for its long coastline of fine sand and turquoise blue waters. The city itself is a lively centre with a mix of modern hotels, restaurants and vibrant markets. Nha Trang is popular not only with tourists, but also with locals who frequent the beaches on weekends and holidays.

Both places offer a wealth of water sports, including snorkeling, diving, jet skiing, and boat trips to nearby islands. Phú Quốc is also known for its fishing and pearl farming industries, which visitors can explore to learn about traditional Vietnamese handicrafts. In Nha Trang, in addition to the beaches, visitors will also find historical landmarks such as the Po Nagar Cham temple complex, which offers insight into the rich history and culture of the region.

The beaches of Phú Quốc and Nha Trang are known not only for their natural beauty, but also for their gastronomic diversity. Visitors can sample fresh seafood and local specialties offered in the numerous restaurants along the coast. Sunsets over the ocean are an unforgettable experience that invites visitors to fully enjoy the beauty and serenity of these tropical paradises.

The traditional Tet festival: Vietnamese New Year

The traditional Tet festival, the Vietnamese New Year, is the most important and significant festival in Vietnam, celebrated every year according to the lunar calendar. It marks the beginning of the new year and falls in the period between the end of January and mid-February according to the Western calendar. Tet is not only a time of festive celebrations, but also a time of family, traditions and respect for ancestors.

Preparations for Tet begin weeks in advance, as people clean and decorate their homes to say goodbye to the old year and welcome the new year. The house is decorated with kumquat trees and peach blossoms, which are considered symbols of good luck and prosperity. People buy new clothes and prepare special dishes that are served during the festival.

Traditional dishes include bánh chưng (pressed pork pie), bánh tét (cylindrical rice cake), and various types of pickled vegetables. These dishes have symbolic meanings and are said to bring good luck, prosperity and health for the coming year. During Tet, it is also customary to show respect to the ancestors by erecting altars in the houses and performing rites such as burning incense and offering offerings.

One of the central traditions of Tet is the custom of the Red Envelopes (Lì Xì), in which gifts of money are given as blessings and congratulations, especially to children. This gesture symbolizes prosperity and is intended to protect recipients in the new year.

During the Tet Festival, public events and performances are also held, including dragon dances, lion dances, and traditional musical performances. These celebrations draw crowds and add to the festive atmosphere that engulfs the entire country.

Tet is not only a time of celebration, but also a time of reflection and new beginnings. Family members who have moved to the cities or abroad often return home to spend the holidays with their loved ones. The time around Tet is therefore also characterized by travel, traffic and a feeling of togetherness among people.

For the Vietnamese, the traditional Tet festival is more than just a holiday; it is a deeply cultural heritage that celebrates the values of family, unity and respect for the past. It is an opportunity to experience and understand Vietnam's rich cultural identity, which comes alive in this significant annual event.

The Art of Water Puppet Theatre

The Water Puppet Theatre, or "Múa rối nước", is a unique form of traditional Vietnamese puppet theatre that has been practiced in Vietnam for centuries. It has its roots in the rice fields of northern Vietnam, especially in the provinces around Hanoi, and is deeply rooted in the country's folklore and culture.

The special feature of the water puppet theatre is that the puppets act on a water surface, which gives the whole thing a magical and almost magical quality. The performances traditionally take place on large water stages, which are often designed like a rice field. The puppets themselves are carved from wood and have movable limbs that are manipulated by experienced puppeteers under the water's surface. These puppeteers stand behind a bamboo curtain, which often serves as part of the stage, and hide their movements from the audience.

The themes of the water puppet plays often reflect rural life and tell stories from Vietnamese history, folklore and legends. They can be humorous, dramatic, or educational, and performances are often accompanied by live music that includes traditional Vietnamese instruments such as the đàn bầu (a one-stringed monochord) and the đàn nhị (a two-stringed fiddle). This music enhances the atmosphere of the performance and contributes to the narrative.

The art of water puppet theatre requires both skill and years of experience from the puppeteers, which is often passed down from generation to generation. The puppets must be manipulated with precision and empathy to create vibrant and engaging characters that capture the imagination of the audience.

In recent decades, the water puppet theatre has gained international fame and is performed not only in Vietnam, but also on stages worldwide. It has become a cultural icon of Vietnam, attracting both tourists and locals who want to appreciate and experience the country's traditional arts.

The water puppet theater is not only a form of entertainment, but also a window into Vietnam's rich cultural heritage, which is brought to life in a unique way through the art of puppetry. It remains a fascinating and indispensable element of Vietnamese culture that reflects the artistry and creativity of the people of Vietnam.

The Bat-Trang pottery: craft traditions

Bat Trang pottery is an important craft tradition in Vietnam and has its origins in the village of the same name, Bat Trang, located just a few kilometers from the capital Hanoi. This ceramic tradition has a long history, dating back to the 14th century during the Ly Dynasty.

The Bat Trang region is known for its high-quality ceramics, which are used in everyday life as well as for ceremonial and decorative purposes. The art of Bat-Trang pottery is passed down from generation to generation within families and combines craftsmanship, artistic design and local creativity.

Typical products of Bat-Trang ceramics include vases, bowls, plates, cups, jugs and decorative objects. The ceramics are made from special clays found in the Bat Trang area, which are prized for their quality and durability. Pottery begins with choosing the right clay, which is then hand-shaped by experienced potters or turned on the potter's wheel to get the desired shape.

A characteristic feature of Bat-Trang ceramics is their glazed surface, which is often decorated with traditional patterns and motifs. These embellishments can range from floral patterns to geometric designs to abstract depictions that reflect the artistic diversity and cultural richness of Vietnam.

The production of bat-trang ceramics requires precise craftsmanship and patience throughout the process, including shaping, drying, firing and glazing. Firing is carried out in special furnaces that harden the ceramic at high temperatures, ensuring its strength and durability.

Bat-Trang pottery is not only a craft but also a cultural heritage that makes an important contribution to Vietnamese art and culture. The ceramics from Bat Trang are not only highly appreciated in Vietnam, but have also gained international recognition and are appreciated worldwide for their beauty and quality.

The tradition of bat trang pottery shows the Vietnamese people's attachment to their cultural heritage and their ability to preserve and develop traditional craft techniques through the ages. It remains a living symbol of Vietnam's craftsmanship and cultural identity, celebrating the skill and creative talent of local artists and craftsmen.

Language and script in Vietnam

The Vietnamese language and script form a fascinating and unique system that is deeply rooted in the history and culture of Vietnam. The country's official language is Vietnamese, which is spoken by around 95% of the population and varies in different dialects and accents depending on the region. Vietnamese belongs to the Austroasiatic language family and uses a Latin alphabet based on the alphabet introduced by French missionaries in the 17th century.

The Vietnamese alphabet, also known as Chữ Quốc ngữ, consists of 29 letters, including 22 consonants and 7 vowels. The characters are phonetic and reflect spoken language, making them easier to read for speakers of other Latin alphabet-based languages. Each letter can be combined with different diacritics to indicate the pitch and stress of the syllables, which is important because Vietnamese is a tonal language that uses six different tones to change the meaning of a word.

In addition to the Latin alphabet, there is also the traditional Chinese script, called Han-Nom, which dates back to the 13th century and includes historical texts as well as literary works. Although Han-Nom is less common today than Chữ Quốc ngữ, it is still a significant cultural heritage and a testament to Vietnam's historical ties with China.

The Vietnamese language has absorbed various influences from other languages and cultures throughout history, including Chinese, French, and Khmer. This is reflected not only in the lexicon, but also in the culture and society, which have produced a rich and diverse linguistic heritage.

The importance of language in Vietnam goes beyond communication and is closely linked to national identity and cultural self-image. It serves as a means of preserving and passing on traditions, values and stories from generation to generation.

In recent decades, the Vietnamese education system has developed a lot, which has led to a high literacy rate in the country. The promotion of the Vietnamese language and script is supported by government programs and initiatives that help strengthen the language as the key to national unity and development.

Overall, the Vietnamese language and script remain an integral part of Vietnam's cultural and national identity, not only reflecting the diversity and complexity of the country's linguistic landscape, but also keeping its rich history and cultural heritage alive.

Travel preparation and useful tips

Preparing for travel to Vietnam requires careful planning and consideration of various aspects to ensure a smooth and enjoyable stay. Here are some useful tips and information that can help you prepare for your trip:

1. **Visa and Entry**: A visa is required for most foreign visitors, which must be applied for in advance at a Vietnamese embassy or online. There are different types of visas depending on the length of stay and the purpose of the trip.
2. **Health and vaccinations**: It is recommended to consult your doctor or a travel vaccination center before departure to ensure that all necessary vaccinations are up to date. Particular attention should be paid to vaccinations against hepatitis A and B, typhoid fever and rabies.
3. **Weather and best time to visit**: Vietnam has three main climate zones - northern subtropical, central tropical and southern tropical. The best time to travel varies depending on the region. In general, the months from November to April are best suited for central and southern Vietnam, while

the north offers favorable conditions between October and March.
4. **Clothing and equipment**: Due to the different climate conditions, travelers should bring light cotton clothing for hot and humid conditions, as well as warmer clothing for cool evenings in mountainous regions, depending on the time of travel and destination. Comfortable shoes are important for sightseeing and hiking.
5. **Currency and money**: The official currency in Vietnam is the Vietnamese dong (VND). It is advisable to bring some dong in cash, as small shops and local markets may not accept credit cards. Currency exchange is possible in banks, hotels and authorized currency exchange offices.
6. **Language and communication**: While English is widely spoken in tourist areas and large cities, it is helpful to learn some basic Vietnamese phrases to facilitate interaction with locals and deepen cultural understanding.
7. **Safety and emergency contacts**: Vietnam is generally a safe country to visit, however, travelers should take basic safety precautions, especially when handling personal belongings

and crossing roads. Emergency contacts such as the local police (113) and medical emergency calls (115) should be known.

8. **Transportation and Transportation**: Vietnam has a well-developed transportation system consisting of buses, trains, and domestic flights. It is advisable to book transport in advance, especially during the high season. Taxis and motorcycle taxis are common in urban areas, with pre-trip price negotiation common.

9. **Cultural sensitivity**: Respect for local customs and traditions is important. Especially in religious sites, appropriate clothing and behavior should be observed. Photographing people without their consent should be avoided, as well as entering houses or temples with shoes.

10. **Culinary delights**: Vietnam is famous for its diverse and delicious cuisine. Sample local specialties such as pho (noodle soup), banh mi (sandwiches), and fresh seafood. Street stalls often offer delicious street food that is safe when freshly prepared.

Preparing for a trip to Vietnam requires mindfulness and preparation to fully enjoy the diverse culture, stunning scenery and hospitality of the people. With this information, travelers can make the most of their experience in this fascinating country.

Closing remarks

The conclusion of a book on Vietnam is an opportunity to summarize the broad themes and aspects covered in the previous chapters and to provide a concluding thought. Vietnam, with its rich history, fascinating culture and breathtaking landscapes, remains a country of great diversity and deep resonance.

In this book, we explored the geography of Vietnam, from the majestic mountains in the north to the fertile Mekong Delta plains in the south. We looked at the country's long and complex history, from the early kingdoms to colonization and the Vietnam War that shaped the country's destiny in the 20th century.

The cultural splendor of Vietnam was highlighted by looking at its art, literature, music, and traditional crafts. The unique cuisine, which is characterized by fresh ingredients and aromatic spices, reflects not only the taste, but also the diversity and history of the country.

Vietnam's dynamic development in the 21st century is reflected in its economic boom, its increasing international importance and its efforts to protect the environment and sustainability. The country's political system and its current developments shed light on the challenges and opportunities of a modern society in constant change.

The travel preparations and useful tips have shown that Vietnam is a country to discover and experience, with a hospitality that never ceases to delight its visitors. Although this book could only offer a glimpse into the depth and breadth of Vietnam, I hope it has piqued your curiosity and encouraged you to explore this fascinating country in person.

In the end, Vietnam remains not just a place on the map, but a living mosaic of history, culture and nature that inspires every visitor with its beauty and diversity. May this book help to deepen your understanding and appreciation of Vietnam and give you unforgettable insights into this unique country.

Printed in Great Britain
by Amazon